How to Assess and Interpret Survey Psychometrics

2nd edition

I0964088

THE SURVEY KIT, Second Edition

Purposes: The purposes of this 10-volume Kit are to enable readers to prepare and conduct surveys and to help readers become better users of survey results. Surveys are conducted to collect information; surveyors ask questions of people on the telephone, face-to-face, and by mail. The questions can be about attitudes, beliefs, and behavior as well as socioeconomic and health status. To do a good survey, one must know how to plan and budget for all survey tasks, how to ask questions, how to design the survey (research) project, how to sample respondents, how to collect reliable and valid information, and how to analyze and report the results.

Users: The Kit is for students in undergraduate and graduate classes in the social and health sciences and for individuals in the public and private sectors who are responsible for conducting and using surveys. Its primary goal is to enable users to prepare surveys and collect data that are accurate and useful for primarily practical purposes. Sometimes, these practical purposes overlap with the objectives of scientific research, and so survey researchers will also find the Kit useful.

Format of the Kit: All books in the series contain instructional objectives, exercises and answers, examples of surveys in use and illustrations of survey questions, guidelines for action, checklists of dos and don'ts, and annotated references.

Volumes in The Survey Kit:

1. **The Survey Handbook, 2nd**
   Arlene Fink
2. **How to Ask Survey Questions, 2nd**
   Arlene Fink
3. **How to Conduct Self-Administered and Mail Surveys, 2nd**
   Linda B. Bourque and Eve P. Fielder
4. **How to Conduct Telephone Surveys, 2nd**
   Linda B. Bourque and Eve P. Fielder
5. **How to Conduct In-Person Interviews for Surveys, 2nd**
   Sabine Mertens Oishi
6. **How to Design Survey Studies, 2nd**
   Arlene Fink
7. **How to Sample in Surveys, 2nd**
   Arlene Fink
8. **How to Assess and Interpret Survey Psychometrics, 2nd**
   Mark S. Litwin
9. **How to Manage, Analyze, and Interpret Survey Data, 2nd**
   Arlene Fink
10. **How to Report on Surveys, 2nd**
    Arlene Fink

Mark S. Litwin

How to Assess and Interpret Survey Psychometrics

2nd edition

THE SURVEY KIT

SAGE Publications
International Educational and Professional Publisher
Thousand Oaks ▪ London ▪ New Delhi

For information:

Sage Publications, Inc.
2455 Teller Road
Thousand Oaks, California 91320
E-mail: order@sagepub.com

Sage Publications Ltd.
6 Bonhill Street
London EC2A 4PU
United Kingdom

Sage Publications India Pvt. Ltd.
M-32 Market
Greater Kailash I
New Delhi 110 048 India

Printed in the United States of America

Library of Congress Cataloging-in-Publication Data

The survey kit.—2nd ed.
    p. cm.
Includes bibliographical references.
ISBN 0-7619-2510-4 (set : pbk.)
1. Social surveys. 2. Health surveys. I. Fink, Arlene.
HN29 .S724 2002
300'.723—dc21   2002012405

This book is printed on acid-free paper.

02 03 04 05 10 9 8 7 6 5 4 3 2 1

Acquisitions Editor:	C. Deborah Laughton
Editorial Assistant:	Veronica Novak
Copy Editor:	Judy Selhorst
Production Editor:	Diane S. Foster
Typesetter:	Bramble Books
Proofreader:	Cheryl Rivard
Cover Designer:	Ravi Balasuriya
Production Designer:	Michelle Lee

Contents

How to Assess and Interpret
Survey Psychometrics: Learning Objectives

This book is intended to guide you in assessing and interpreting the quality of collected survey data by thoroughly examining the **survey instrument** used. It also addresses important considerations in the coding and pilot testing of surveys. The specific objectives are as follows:

- Select and apply reliability criteria, including the following:

  – Test-retest reliability
  – Alternate-form reliability
  – Internal consistency reliability
  – Interobserver reliability
  – Intraobserver reliability

- Select and apply validity criteria, including the following:

  – Face validity
  – Content validity
  – Criterion validity
  – Construct validity

- Outline the fundamental principles of scaling and scoring

- Create and use a codebook for survey data

- Pilot-test new and established surveys

- Address cross-cultural issues in survey research

1 Psychometrics

A successful data collection survey is much more than a set of well-designed questions that are written down and administered to a sample population. There are good surveys and bad surveys. Bad surveys produce bad data—that is, data that are unreliable, irreproducible, or invalid, or that waste resources. Good surveys, on the other hand, can yield critical information and provide important windows into the heart of the topic of interest.

Psychometrics is the branch of survey research that enables you to determine how good your survey is. Psychometric principles were originally developed in the field of measurement psychology, but they have been borrowed by many other disciplines. Psychometrics provides survey researchers with a way to quantify the precision of the measurement of qualitative concepts, such as consumer satisfaction, depression, and marital interaction. These phenomena are inherently more difficult to measure than are discrete variables such as a person's zip code, marital status, or height. Example 1.1 presents two surveys of hotel guest satisfaction. It is not obvious whether one or the other is better, but the two are clearly different and will yield different data. The aim of this book is to teach you how to evaluate differences in surveys such as these.

EXAMPLE 1.1
Two Surveys of Hotel Guest Satisfaction

Purpose of the survey: To assess guest satisfaction at a downtown hotel with a 3-**item** survey at the time of checkout.

Survey 1: Circle one number for each item.

1. Did you enjoy your stay?

    Yes. 1
    No 2

2. How good was the service at the hotel?

    Good. 1
    Poor 2

3. Would you stay here again?

    Yes 1
    No. 2

Survey 2: Circle one number for each item.

1. Overall, considering the service, food, and all other aspects of our hotel, how would you describe your stay here?

    Very enjoyable 1
    Somewhat enjoyable 2
    Neither enjoyable nor unenjoyable 3
    Somewhat unenjoyable 4
    Very unenjoyable 5

2. How would you describe our service?

    More efficient than other hotels
       I have stayed in 1

Example 1.1 continued

Equally efficient to other hotels
I have stayed in 2
Less efficient than other hotels
I have stayed in 3

3. How likely are you to stay here again?

Highly likely 1
Likely 2
Not sure 3
Unlikely 4
Highly unlikely 5

Which of the two surveys in Example 1.1 is better? Survey 2 appears as though it might produce more useful information because it provides more than just the yes/no-type questions we see in Survey 1. But perhaps the simplicity of Survey 1 will encourage more hotel guests to complete it. Perhaps only the guests who really hated their stays will take the time to complete Survey 2, causing results that overlook the guests who really enjoyed their stays. Perhaps business guests are the hotel's most important customers, but because they are in a greater rush than pleasure travelers to catch their flights, they are much less likely to take the time at checkout to complete Survey 2. So we really don't know quantitatively which survey is better. What exactly do we mean by *better*? The better survey will more accurately measure guest satisfaction, producing more useful data from which to draw conclusions about the hotel's performance.

Strictly speaking, it is difficult to assess the quality of the data we collect. It is easier to assess the accuracy of the survey instrument that is used to collect those data. This assessment consists primarily of looking at the reliability and the validity of the survey instrument. Example 1.2 demonstrates that different tools used to measure electrical resistance may produce completely different results. The only way to determine which, if either, is correct is by looking directly at the accuracy of the measurement tools and at potential sources of measurement error, such as response variation and non-response.

The resistance meters in Example 1.2 demonstrate an important concept. Before we can use a survey instrument to collect meaningful data, we must test it to ensure its accuracy. This is true regardless of whether we are dealing with resistance meters, guest satisfaction questionnaires, marketing surveys, crime assessments, depression scales, or any other survey instrument. What matters is not how quantitative the data are but how well the survey instrument performs. In Chapters 2 and 3 of this book, which address the reliability and the validity of survey instruments, this idea is explored in greater detail.

EXAMPLE 1.2
Resistance Meters

Two licensed electricians use different resistance meters to measure the ohms in four brand-new circuits during a new product analysis. Pat uses the old meter she has been using for the past 15 years. Jerry uses a new model that he just bought from HomeLine, Inc., a reputable mail-order company. After they take their measurements, Pat's data are 6, 16, 38, and 119 ohms, and Jerry's data are 19, 28, 73, and 184 ohms. Since there is no way to determine which, if either, data set is correct, we must assess the accuracy of the resistance meters themselves. We do this by asking both Pat and Jerry to measure the resistance in a series of quality-control circuits in which the ohms are known with certainty in advance. After Pat and Jerry measure the resistance three different times in the quality-control circuits, we find Pat's meter to be more accurate. Therefore, we use her data in the new product analysis of the four new circuits.

2 Reliability

In any set of data we collect, there will be some amount of error. Naturally, we want to minimize this error so that the data provide as accurate a reflection of the truth as possible.

In survey research, error comprises two components: random error and measurement error. **Random error** is the unpredictable error that occurs in all research. It may be caused by many different factors, but it is affected primarily by sampling techniques. To lower the chance of random error, we could select a larger and more representative sample. Collecting a larger sample will increase the cost of the study, however, so it is often neither practical nor feasible. Instead, we could use statistics to calculate the probability that a particular result is due to random error. If that probability falls below the limit we set, then we "reject the null hypothesis" and draw inferences about our population. (Recall that in statistical analysis, we make a conservative assumption, called the *null hypothesis*, that our two groups of interest do not differ in the particular variable we are studying. For instance, if we were comparing men's and women's responses to the surveys in Example 1.1 concerning hotel guest satisfaction, the null hypothesis would be that there is no difference. We would design the survey research to test that null hypothesis and see if we could reasonably reject it, thus allowing us to draw inferences about differences between male and female hotel guests. (For more information on hypothesis testing, see **How to Manage, Analyze, and Interpret Survey Data,** Volume 9 in this series.)

Measurement error refers to how well or poorly a particular instrument performs in a given population. No instrument is perfect, so we always expect at least some error to occur during the measurement process. For example, a stopwatch with a minute hand but no second hand cannot measure runners' times in a 5-kilometer race to the nearest second; the best it can do is count minutes. Differences of less than 60 seconds in the runners' times will be lost in the measurement error of the stopwatch. The smaller the measurement error, the closer our data are to the truth. However, even when random error is thought to be zero, some measurement error will occur. This measurement error reflects the precision (or lack of precision) of the survey instrument itself.

Reliability is a statistical measure of the reproducibility or stability of the data gathered by the survey instrument. Example 2.1 illustrates the principle of reliability with a comparison of two different tools used to measure fabric. In the example, the metal yardsticks used at Honor Guard are more reliable and have less measurement error than the rubber tape measures used at Notso. Thus Honor Guard's results are a more accurate reflection of the truth. Even so, there may still be some degree of measurement error. If the salesperson at Honor Guard doesn't see very well and cannot read the difference between 36 inches and 35 inches, then Lane may still get shorted. Neither the metal yardsticks nor the rubber tape measures are perfectly reliable, and there is always some possibility of measurement error.

EXAMPLE 2.1
Fabric Measurement

Honor Guard Fabric Company sells its fabric by the yard and uses expensive aluminum yardsticks to quantify the amount of each purchase. Notso Fabrics also sells its fabric by the yard but uses tape measures made from inexpensive thin rubber strips to measure its quantities. Lane needs exactly 3 yards of blue cotton fabric to make a set of bumpers for his twins' cribs. At Notso, Lane has found over the years that the lengths of measured fabric are inconsistent. Because the rubber tape measures can be stretched to varying degrees, depending on the strength of the salesperson, a "yard" of fabric sold at Notso may actually be anywhere from 35 inches to 41 inches long. At Honor Guard, all measured yards of fabric are always very nearly the same length; the measurements vary only with the visual acuity of the salesperson. Lane goes to Honor Guard for his purchase, because he knows that there, a yard is always a yard.

Types of Reliability

No survey instrument or test is perfectly reliable, but some are clearly more reliable than others. When evaluating the value of a data set, we begin by looking at the reliability characteristics of the measurement instrument. Reliability is commonly assessed in three forms: test-retest, alternate-form, and internal consistency. Intraobserver and interobserver reliability are also addressed below.

TEST-RETEST RELIABILITY

Test-retest reliability is the most commonly used indicator of survey instrument reliability. It is a measure of how reproducible a set of results is. Survey researchers test a survey instrument by having the same respondents complete the instrument at two different points in time to see how stable their responses are. They then calculate **correlation coefficients**, or *r* **values**, to compare the two sets of responses. (See **How to Manage, Analyze, and Interpret Survey Data,** Volume 9 in this series.) These correlation coefficients are collectively referred to as the survey instrument's test-retest reliability. In general, the correlation coefficients are considered good if they are at least 0.70. This implies that the survey responses are reasonably consistent from one point in time to another.

Sometimes data are not collected from a group of subjects but are recorded by one observer. In such a case, the survey researcher assesses test-retest reliability by having that individual make two separate measurements. The researcher then compares the two data sets from the same observer. The correlation between two data sets from the same individual is commonly known as **intraobserver reliability.** This measure of the stability of responses from the same respondent is a form of test-retest reliability.

In Example 2.2, the measurement of test-retest reliability is demonstrated in a survey item that asks about crime rates in different cities. Example 2.3 presents a situation where test-retest reliability is low in a survey item that asks about education attitudes in the same respondents as those in Example 2.2.

EXAMPLE 2.2
Test-Retest Reliability: Crime Rates

Adam has designed a new survey instrument to measure grand larceny rates in a group of urban centers at high risk for various types of crime. One of the items on the survey asks the deputy chief of police in each urban center whether grand larceny rates have been mild, moder-

Example 2.2 continued

ate, or severe during the past month. In order to gauge whether respondents' answers to this item are consistent over time, Adam administers the survey instrument once to a sample of 50 deputy police chiefs in different urban centers and records the data. He then administers the identical survey instrument a second time, 4 weeks later, to the same 50 deputy police chiefs and records those data. Because actual grand larceny rates tend to be stable over short periods of time, Adam expects that any differences in the survey responses will reflect measurement error of the survey instrument and not actual changes in the crime rates. When Adam compares the sets of data from the two different time points, he finds that the correlation coefficient is 0.89. He knows that this item produces responses that are stable over moderate time periods, because the correlation coefficient exceeds 0.70. Therefore, his item has good test-retest reliability.

EXAMPLE 2.3
Test-Retest Reliability: Education Attitudes

Adam also wants to assess attitudes in the same deputy police chiefs to find out whether their police school curricula adequately prepared them to avoid professional burnout, a common problem among law enforcement officers. He designs a 3-item survey that asks how extensive their police training in avoiding professional burnout was, how relevant those lessons are at present, and how easy it is to put those techniques into practice. He administers the same 3-item attitude survey at two time points 4 weeks apart but finds that the correlation

Example 2.3 continued

coefficients for the items are only 0.32, 0.12, and 0.17 respectively. Adam thus concludes that this survey does not produce responses that are stable over time; he realizes that the deputy police chiefs' attitudes about their training may be subject to recall bias and are likely to change from week to week. Various factors may be influencing the changing responses. Perhaps the education attitudes are not dependent only on the quality of the education. Perhaps the attitudes are more related to salary or to how surly the boss is acting on any given day. Perhaps there are other factors influencing education attitudes in this population. Because Adam does not know what these other factors are, he cannot control for them. He is forced to drop these items because their test-retest reliability is too low.

You can calculate test-retest reliability not only for single items, but also for groups of items. In fact, test-retest reliability is most often reported for entire survey instruments or for scales (more on scales in Chapter 4) within survey instruments. Example 2.4 demonstrates test-retest reliability in a series of written items that are administered together to measure pain in men undergoing hernia surgery.

EXAMPLE 2.4
Test-Retest Reliability: A Pain Scale

Jackie wants to measure postoperative pain in a group of 12 adult men undergoing hernia surgery. She designs a series of 4 separate items to assess the pain in terms of its intensity, quality, impact, and duration over the past 10 minutes, each rated as a number from 1 to 10. She cre-

Example 2.4 continued

ates a score for the 4-item scale by summing the responses to the items. She administers the survey instrument 2 hours after surgery (Time 1) and again 4 hours after surgery (Time 2), two points when pain levels should be similar. She then compares the two sets of pain scale scores by calculating a correlation coefficient and finds it to be 0.79. She concludes that her pain scale has good test-retest reliability during the immediate postoperative period in this population.

When measuring test-retest reliability, you must be careful not to select items or scales that measure variables that are likely to change over short periods of time. Variables that are likely to change over a given period of time will produce low test-retest reliability in measurement instruments. This does not mean that the survey instrument is performing poorly; it simply means that the attribute itself has changed. Example 2.5 illustrates how to select an appropriate time interval over which to assess test-retest reliability.

EXAMPLE 2.5
Test-Retest Reliability: Anxiety

Len uses a well-known short survey instrument to measure anxiety in a group of college students before and after midterm examinations. He administers the items 4 days prior to the exams (Time 1), 3 days prior to the exams (Time 2), and 2 days after the exams (Time 3). He calculates the correlation coefficient between Times 1 and 2 to be 0.84, the correlation coefficient between Times 1 and 3 to be 0.12, and the correlation coefficient between Times 2 and 3 to be 0.09. The correct test-retest reliability figure for Len to report is 0.84. This reflects

Example 2.5 continued

the stability of the responses to the survey instrument during a period when Len would expect the responses to remain fairly stable. Len deduces that the other two figures represent true changes in anxiety levels and not poor test-retest reliability. Based on his reliable survey instrument, he concludes that anxiety levels go down after exams.

Len's colleague, Bryan, designs his own new survey instrument to measure anxiety in the same group of college students at the same time points. His correlation coefficients are 0.34, 0.43, and 0.50, respectively. Bryan cannot make any sound deductions about anxiety levels because his survey instrument does not have good test-retest reliability.

You can certainly measure characteristics that tend to change over time. In fact, this is often the purpose of survey research. But test-retest reliability must be documented over shorter periods to decrease the degree of measurement error attributable to the survey itself. When measuring test-retest reliability, you must also consider that individuals may become familiar with the items and so may answer partly based on their memory of what they answered the previous time. This phenomenon, called the **practice effect**, presents a challenging problem that must be addressed in measures of test-retest reliability over short periods of time. As a result of the practice effect, test-retest reliability figures can be falsely inflated.

ALTERNATE-FORM RELIABILITY

Alternate-form reliability provides one way to escape the problem of the practice effect. It involves using differently worded items to measure the same attributes. Questions and responses are reworded or their order is changed so that items are similar but not identical. When you are testing reliability using this method, you must be careful to create items that address the exact same aspect of behavior and also use the same vocabulary level and have the same level of difficulty. The items must differ only in their wording. You then administer the items or scales to the same population at different time points and calculate the correlation coefficients. If these are high, the survey instrument or item is said to have good alternate-form reliability. One common way to test alternate-form reliability is simply to change the order of the response set. Example 2.6 shows two differently ordered response sets for the same item question. Either response set can be used without changing the meaning of the question.

EXAMPLE 2.6
Alternate-Form Reliability:
Response Sets for Depression

The following are equivalent but differently ordered response sets to single items on depression. For each of these three items, the two response sets differ only in their sequence. They are good items for this method of measuring alternate-form reliability.

Item 1: Circle one number in each response set.

Version A

How often during the past 4 weeks have you felt sad and blue?

Example 2.6 continued

All of the time 1
Most of the time 2
Some of the time. 3
Occasionally 4
Never. 5

Version B

How often during the past 4 weeks have you felt sad and blue?

Never. 1
Occasionally 2
Some of the time. 3
Most of the time 4
All of the time 5

Item 2: *Circle one number in each response set.*

Version A

During the past 4 weeks, I have felt downhearted

Every day . . . 1
Some days. . . 2
Never 3

Version B

During the past 4 weeks, I have felt downhearted

Never 1
Some days. . . 2
Every day . . . 3

Item 3: *Circle one number in each response set.*

Example 2.6 continued

Version A

During the past 4 weeks, have you felt like hurting your-self?

    Yes. 1
    No. 2

Version B

During the past 4 weeks, have you felt like hurting your-self?

    No. 1
    Yes. 2

Changing the order of the response sets is most effective when the two time points for administration of the items are close together. This approach forces respondents to read the items and response sets very carefully, thereby decreasing the practice effect. Another way to test alternate-form reliability is to change the wording of the response sets without changing the meaning. Example 2.7 presents two items on urinary function, each with two different response sets that collect the same information with different but synonymous wording.

EXAMPLE 2.7
Alternate-Form Reliability:
Response Set Wording

The following are equivalent but differently worded response sets to two single items on urinary function. The response sets for each item are differently worded

Example 2.7 continued

but functionally equivalent. This makes them good candidates for use in a test of alternate-form reliability.

Item 1: *Circle one number in each response set.*

Version A

During the past week, how often did you usually empty your bladder?

1 to 2 times per day	1
3 to 4 times per day	2
5 to 8 times per day	3
12 times per day	4
More than 12 times per day	5

Version B

During the past week, how often did you usually empty your bladder?

Every 12 to 24 hours	1
Every 6 to 8 hours	2
Every 3 to 5 hours	3
Every 2 hours	4
More than every 2 hours	5

Item 2: *Circle one number in each response set.*

Version A

During the past 4 weeks, how much did you leak urine?

Never	1
A little bit	2
A moderate amount	3
A lot	4
Constantly	5

Example 2.7 continued

Version B

During the past 4 weeks, how much did you leak urine?

I used no pads in my underwear . . . 1
I used 1 pad per day 2
I used 2 to 3 pads per day 3
I used 4 to 6 pads per day 4
I used 7 or more pads per day 5

Another common method used to test alternate-form reliability is to change the actual wording of the items themselves. Again, if you use this method, you must be very careful to design items that are truly equivalent to each other. Items that are worded with different degrees of difficulty do not measure the same attribute. They are more likely to measure the reading comprehension or cognitive function of the respondent. Example 2.8 contains two questions that are *not* equivalent even though they are about the same topic. The items in this example would *not* provide a good test of alternate-form reliability. Despite the same response sets, these two versions are *not* equivalent and therefore *cannot* be used to test alternate-form reliability.

EXAMPLE 2.8
Nonequivalent Item Rewording

The following are differently worded versions of the same item intended to measure assertiveness at work. If you look closely at the wording, you can see that the two versions do ask basically the same question. In fact, the response sets are identical. But the two items are clearly *not* equivalent because their vocabulary levels are

Example 2.8 continued

profoundly different. They would *not* be good items with which to test alternate-form reliability. The first is a measure of assertiveness, whereas the second is as much a measure of reading comprehension as of assertiveness.

Item 1: Circle one number.

When your boss blames you for something you did not do, how often do you stick up for yourself?

> All of the tim 1
> Some of the time 2
> None of the time 3

Item 2: Circle one number.

When presented with difficult professional situations in which a superior censures you for an act for which you are not responsible, how frequently do you respond in an assertive way?

> All of the tim 1
> Some of the time 2
> None of the time 3

Example 2.9 displays two questions on the same subject that are also differently worded, but these two *are* equivalent and *can* be used to test alternate-form reliability. Notice that even though the response sets are different, the items are much closer in style and reading level than those in Example 2.8.

When testing alternate-form reliability, you can administer the different forms at separate time points to the same population, or if the sample is large enough, you can divide it in half and administer each of the two alternate forms to half of the group. You would then compare the results from the two halves. This technique, called the **split-halves**

EXAMPLE 2.9
Equivalent Item Rewording: Depression

The following are equivalent but differently worded items that measure loneliness. Notice that although the items are worded differently and have different response sets, they ask about the exact same issue in very similar ways. A high correlation coefficient, or *r* value, between the responses to these two items would indicate that the item has good alternate-form reliability.

Item 1: Circle one number.

How often in the past month have you felt all alone in the world?

    Every day 1
    Some days 2
    Occasionally 3
    Never 4

Item 2: Circle one number.

During the past 4 weeks, how often have you felt a sense of loneliness?

    All of the time 1
    Sometimes 2
    From time to time . . 3
    Never 4

method, is generally accepted as being as good as administering the different forms to the same sample at different time points. When you use the split-halves method, you must make sure that you select the halves of the sample randomly. You must also measure the sociodemographic characteristics of both halves of the sample to make sure there are no group differences that might account for any disparities in the two data sets. Such unintended group differences can bias the results, and you may need to adjust or correct for them in a multivariate analysis.

Although all the examples presented above have used two different item wordings, two response sets, or large samples divided in two, there is no rule that limits the number to two. If your sample is large enough, you can use three, four, or more subsamples to test alternate forms of an item. If you do so, however, you must check your sample sizes to make sure you have enough statistical power to show any difference in the alternate forms. (For more on statistical power, see **How to Sample in Surveys**, Volume 7 in this series.)

INTERNAL CONSISTENCY RELIABILITY

Internal consistency reliability is another psychometric measure that is commonly used in the assessment of survey instruments and scales. It is applied not to single items but to groups of items that are thought to measure different aspects of the same concept. Internal consistency is an indicator of how well the different items measure the same issue. This is important because a group of items that purports to measure one variable should indeed be clearly focused on that variable. Although single items may be quicker and less expensive to administer, your data set will be richer and more reliable if you use several different items to gain information about a particular behavior or topic. Example 2.10 contains a real scale that is used in medical survey research today. It has been shown to have very high internal consistency reliability.

EXAMPLE 2.10
A Physical Function Scale

In the RAND Medical Outcomes Study (MOS), a large research project conducted in the 1980s, a series of items

Example 2.10 continued

was developed to measure quality of life in patients with various medical conditions. The most popular survey instrument produced in the MOS is called the RAND 36-Item Health Survey (alternatively known as the Short Form 36 or SF-36). One of the eight dimensions included in this survey instrument is physical function. Instead of simply choosing one item to assess physical function, the study's authors determined that it was more useful to ask 10 questions about physical function. The scale follows.

The following questions are about activities you might do during a typical day. Does your health now limit you in these activities. If so, how much? *Circle one number on each line.*	Limited a Lot	Limited a Little	Not Limited at All
1. **Vigorous activities**, such as running, lifting heavy objects, participating in strenuous sports	1	2	3
2. **Moderate activities**, such as moving a table, pushing a vacuum cleaner, bowling, or playing golf	1	2	3
3. Lifting or carrying groceries	1	2	3
4. Climbing **several** flights of stairs	1	2	3
5. Climbing **one** flight of stairs	1	2	3
6. Bending, kneeling, or stooping	1	2	3
7. Walking **more than a mile**	1	2	3
8. Walking **several blocks**	1	2	3
9. Walking **one block**	1	2	3
10. Bathing or dressing yourself	1	2	3

Example 2.10 continued

It is easy to see how this series of items provides much more information on physical function than a single item such as the following:

Circle one number.

	Limited a Lot	Limited a Little	Not Limited at All
How limited are you in your day-to-day physical activities?	1	2	3

The measurement of internal consistency involves the calculation of a statistic known as Cronbach's coefficient alpha, named for the 20th-century psychometrician who first reported it in 1951. Coefficient alpha measures internal consistency reliability among a group of items that are combined to form a single scale. It is a statistic that reflects the homogeneity of the scale. That is, it is an indication of how well the different items complement each other in their measurement of different aspects of the same variable or quality. The formula for calculating coefficient alpha can be found in any textbook of test theory or psychometric statistics (see also **How to Manage, Analyze, and Interpret Survey Data**, Volume 9 in this series).

Example 2.11 provides a demonstration of coefficient alpha calculation. For simplicity, the example contains a scale with three yes/no items, but coefficient alpha can also be calculated for longer scales containing items with more than two responses (most scales are longer, and most items on most scales have more than two responses). The calculation of coefficient alpha for longer scales is greatly facilitated by a good statistician and a computer.

EXAMPLE 2.11
Calculating Internal Consistency

In the RAND 36-Item Health Survey, emotional well-being is assessed with 5 items, called the Mental Health Index or MHI-5. Suppose we created a smaller mental health scale consisting of the following subset of 3 items and wanted to test its internal consistency reliability.

Circle one number on each line.

During the past month:	Yes	No
Have you been a very nervous person?	1	0
Have you felt downhearted and blue?	1	0
Have you felt so down in the dumps that nothing could cheer you up?	1	0

The response set for each of these items results in a number of points that are summed to form the scale score. A low total score reflects poorer emotional health, and a higher total score indicates better emotional health. For simplicity, the response sets have been reduced to yes/no answers and scored with 1 point for a yes and 0 points for a no.

In order to calculate coefficient alpha, we administer the scale to a sample of five nursing home patients and obtain the following results:

Example 2.11 continued

Patient	Item A	Item B	Item C	Summed Scale Score
1	0	1	1	2
2	1	1	1	3
3	0	0	0	0
4	1	1	1	3
5	1	1	0	2
Percentage positive	3/5 = .6	4/5 = .8	3/5 = .6	

First we must calculate the sample mean and the sample variance (these formulas can be found in any basic statistics text). We also note the percentage of positive responses for each item and that the total number of items in the scale is 3.

Calculations:

The sample mean score is $(2 + 3 + 0 + 3 + 2)/5 = 2$.

The sample variance is

$$\frac{(2-2)^2 + (3-2)^2 + (0-2)^2 + (3-2)^2 + (2-2)^2}{(5-1)} = \frac{6}{4} = 1.5.$$

Coefficient alpha for a series of dichotomous items is

$$\left[1 - \frac{(\% \text{ positive})_i (\% \text{ negative})_i}{\text{Sample variance}}\right] \left[\frac{k}{k-1}\right]$$

as follows (k = number of items in the scale):

$$\left[1 - \frac{1 - (.6)(.4) + (.8)(.2) + (.6)(.4)}{1.5}\right] \left[3/3-1\right] = 0.86$$

Example 2.11 continued

The internal consistency coefficient alpha is 0.86, suggesting very good reliability in this scale of three dichotomous items.

If a scale's internal consistency reliability is low, you can often improve it by adding more items or by reexamining the existing items for clarity.

Reliability testing of items and scales provides quantitative measurements of how well an instrument performs in a given population. If you develop a new survey instrument, it is imperative that you test it for reliability before you use it to collect actual data from which you will draw inferences. One of the major drawbacks of new survey instruments is that they are often nothing more than collections of questions that seem to the surveyors to fit well together. Even when you are using an established survey instrument with a long and successful track record, it is important that you calculate its internal consistency reliability and, if possible, test-retest reliability to document its performance in your population. Established survey instruments have typically undergone extensive psychometric evaluation, but the original author's sample population may have been quite different from yours. When multicultural issues or language barriers are relevant considerations, it is especially important to carry out reliability testing. If you are collecting data from a group of subjects with whom that survey instrument has not previously been used, you must document how well it performs in the new population by measuring its psychometric properties, including reliability.

INTEROBSERVER RELIABILITY

Interobserver (or interrater) **reliability** provides a measure of how well two or more evaluators agree in their assessment of a variable. It is usually reported as a correlation coefficient between different data collectors. When survey instruments are self-administered and designed to measure the respondents' own behaviors or attitudes, interobserver reliability is not used. However, whenever there is a subjective component in the measurement of an external variable, it is important to calculate this statistic. Sometimes, interobserver reliability is used as a psychometric property of a survey instrument, whereas at other times, it is itself the variable of interest. Example 2.12 demonstrates the measurement of interobserver reliability in a survey designed to measure efficiency in the workplace.

EXAMPLE 2.12
Interobserver Reliability:
Impact of Job Sharing

Dana designs a survey instrument to assess the impact of a new job-sharing policy at a newspaper production plant. The policy allows employees with small children to share a 40-hour workweek to allow each worker more time at home. The survey instrument is a questionnaire completed by a "peer judge," who answers a series of 20 questions on the efficiency of the 100-member workforce on each shift. Dana plans to ask three different workers to act as peer judges and complete the survey instrument by quietly making observations during a regular shift. Dana will figure the efficiency scale score as determined by each peer judge. She will then compare the three data sets by calculating correlation coefficients to determine the interobserver reliability of the survey instrument. If the correlations are high, Dana will know

Example 2.12 continued

that her survey instrument has high reliability from one observer to another. She may conclude that it can be used by various peer judges to measure the impact of the new policy on efficiency in this workforce. If the correlations are low, Dana must consider that the survey instrument may be operator dependent, not a good quality for such a survey. She may then conclude that the survey instrument is not stable among different judges. She may decide to assess the new policy's impact by using one judge for all of the work shifts.

Example 2.13 provides another demonstration that interobserver reliability may be more than a psychometric statistic—it may also be the primary variable of interest. In this example, interobserver reliability is not only a psychometric property of the test, it is an outcome variable of primary interest to the data collectors.

EXAMPLE 2.13
Interobserver Reliability: Mammography

Rose and Max are very interested in determining whether mammography is a good test to diagnose early-stage breast cancer. They design a research project in which they will show the same 10 mammograms to a series of 12 different radiologists. They will ask each radiologist individually to rate each mammogram as suspicious for cancer, indeterminate, or not suspicious for cancer. They will then compare the responses from the 12 radiologists and calculate correlation coefficients. This will provide a measure of interobserver reliability. If

Example 2.13 continued

the correlations are high, Rose and Max will conclude that mammography has a high degree of interobserver reliability, but if they are low, they will conclude that the interobserver reliability of mammography is suspect. Rose and Max plan to report their findings in the medical literature.

Interobserver reliability is often used when the measurement process is less quantitative than the variable being measured. The other forms of reliability discussed in this chapter are more often used when the variable itself is more qualitative. There are, of course, exceptions to this general rule.

Type of Reliability	Characteristics	Comments
Test-retest	Measures the stability of responses over time, typically in the same group of respondents	Requires administration of survey to a sample at two different and appropriate points in time (Time points that are too far apart may produce diminished reliability estimates that reflect actual change over time in the variable of interest.)
Intraobserver	Measures the stability of responses over time in the same individual respondent	Requires completion of a survey by an individual at two different and appropriate points in time (Time points that are too far apart may produce diminished reliability estimates that reflect actual change over time in the variable of interest.)
Alternate-form	Uses differently worded items or response sets to obtain the same information about a specific topic	Requires two items in which the wording is different but aimed at the same specific variable and at the same vocabulary level
Internal consistency	Measures how well several items in a scale vary together in a sample	Usually requires a computer and statistician to carry out calculations
Interobserver	Measures how well two or more different respondents rate the same phenomenon	May be used to demonstrate reliability of a survey or may itself be the variable of interest in a study

NOTE: Reliability is usually expressed as a correlation coefficient, or r value, between two sets of data. Levels of 0.70 or more are generally accepted as representing good reliability.

3 Validity

In addition to determining reliability, you must assess the **validity** of items, scales, and whole survey instruments—that is, how well they measure what they are intended to measure. An item that is supposed to measure pain should measure pain and not some related variable such as anxiety. A scale that claims to measure emotional quality of life should not measure depression, which is a related but different variable. Reliability assessments are necessary, but they are not the whole picture when you examine the psychometric properties of a survey instrument. Once you have documented that a scale is reliable over time and in alternate forms, you must then make sure that it is reliably measuring the truth.

Example 3.1 takes another look at the problem of measuring fabric that we explored in Example 2.1. Before, we were interested in reliability, but now we are concerned with validity.

EXAMPLE 3.1
Fabric Measurement Revisited

Recall from Example 2.1 in Chapter 2 that salespersons at the Honor Guard Fabric Company use expensive aluminum yardsticks to measure the lengths of all the pieces of fabric the company sells. We previously determined that these metal yardsticks are very reliable; that is, they measure out the exact same length of cloth every time. Suppose that during a store audit, Honor Guard finds that each of its "yardsticks" is actually 40 inches long. Every single time a clerk sells a yard of fabric, the measuring stick reliably counts out 40 inches of fabric. The company realizes that over the years, it has given away thousands of inches of extra fabric because its aluminum measuring sticks are too long. Like a broken clock, the measurement instrument is reliable but not valid.

Types of Validity

You must document validity when evaluating new survey instruments or when applying established survey instruments to new populations. Validity is an important measure of a survey instrument's accuracy. Survey researchers typically measure several types of validity when assessing the performance of a survey instrument: face, content, criterion, and construct.

FACE VALIDITY

Face validity is based on a cursory review of items by untrained judges, such as your Auntie Mame, your boyfriend, your roommate's stepfather, or your squash partner. Assessing face validity might involve simply showing your survey to a few untrained individuals to see whether they think the items look all right to them. This measure, which is often confused with content validity, is the least scientific of all the validity measures. Although face and content validity are similar, face validity involves a much more casual assessment of item appropriateness. In fact, many researchers do not consider face validity a measure of validity at all.

CONTENT VALIDITY

Content validity is a subjective measure of how appropriate items or scales seem to a set of reviewers who have some knowledge of the subject matter. The assessment of content validity typically involves an organized review of the survey's contents to ensure that it includes everything it should and does not include anything it should not. If you are examining the content validity of medical scales, for example, it is important that you include actual patients and their families in the evaluation process. Doctors and nurses may be unaware of the subtle nuances perceived by patients who live day to day with medical conditions. Patients' families also may provide helpful insights into dimensions that might be overlooked by "experts." That said, it remains important for clinicians to review the items for relevance to and focus on the variables of interest.

Content validity is not quantified with statistics. Rather, it is presented as an overall opinion of a group of trained judges. Strictly speaking, it is not a scientific measure of a survey instrument's accuracy. Nevertheless, it provides a good foundation on which to build a methodologically rigorous assessment of a survey instrument's validity. Example 3.2 shows how content validity is assessed for a sociological survey on interactions between spouses.

EXAMPLE 3.2
Content Validity: Marital Interaction

Kristen designs a new scale to collect data on marital interaction as a dimension of health-related quality of life. She develops a series of 16 items about spousal communication, interpersonal confidence, and discussions within the marriage. She plans to use her new scale to assess the impact of social support on a large population of married cancer patients who are undergoing a difficult and stressful chemotherapy protocol.

Before administering her new scale, Kristen asks three oncologists, three psychologists, two social workers, an oncology nurse-practitioner, four cancer patients, and two spouses of cancer patients to review each of the items. She asks these reviewers to rate each item and the scale as a whole for appropriateness and relevance to the issue of marital interaction. She also asks each reviewer to list any areas that are pertinent to marital interaction but not covered in the 16 items. Once all the reviews are complete, Kristen studies them to determine whether her new survey instrument has content validity.

If she had wished to assess face validity, Kristen might have asked her college roommate or her grandfather to take a look at the survey and tell her whether the items seemed appropriate. Kristen decides to bypass face validity because she has chosen to look more carefully at content validity and because she knows that face validity is basically worthless.

CRITERION VALIDITY

Criterion validity is a measure of how well one instrument stacks up against another instrument or predictor. It provides much more quantitative evidence on the accuracy of a survey instrument than does content or face validity. It may be measured in various ways, depending on how much previous work is available in the area of study. Criterion validity may be broken down into two components: concurrent validity and predictive validity.

Concurrent Validity

Concurrent validity requires that the survey instrument in question be judged against some other method that is acknowledged as a gold standard for assessing the same variable. This other method may be a published psychometric index, a scientific measurement of some factor, or another generally accepted test. The fundamental requirement is that most survey scholars regard it as a good way to measure the same concept. The statistic is calculated as a correlation coefficient with that test. A high correlation suggests good concurrent validity. Alternatively, a test may be selected for comparison that is expected to measure an attribute or behavior that is opposite to the dimension of interest. In this case, a low correlation indicates good concurrent validity. There are times when you would not simply use an established gold standard as your measure of choice; for instance, the test may be too cumbersome, too expensive, or too invasive to apply.

Example 3.3 demonstrates the use of an established scale to assess concurrent validity in a new scale, and Example 3.4 illustrates the assessment of a new survey instrument's validity in measuring water supply through a comparison with a more standard measure of water supply.

EXAMPLE 3.3
Concurrent Validity: Pain Tolerance

Alisha develops a new 4-item index to assess pain tolerance in a group of patients scheduled for surgery. The items draw information from patients' memories of

Example 3.3 continued

their past experiences with pain. Alisha sums the results from the 4 items to form a Pain Tolerance Index score. The higher the score, the greater the tolerance for pain. The index is self-administered and takes about a minute for a patient to complete. To assess concurrent validity, Alisha administers her 4 items together with a published pain-tolerance survey instrument that has been in use for more than a decade in anesthesiology research and is generally accepted as the gold standard in the field. It contains 45 items, requires an interviewer, and takes an average of an hour to complete. It is also scored as a sum of item responses.

Alisha is able to gather data with both survey instruments in a sample of 24 patients. She calculates the correlation coefficient to be 0.92 between her new test of pain tolerance and the gold-standard test of pain tolerance. She concludes that her index has high concurrent validity with the gold standard. Because hers is much shorter and easier to administer, she convinces the principal investigator in a large national study of postoperative pain to use her more efficient index rather than the older, longer survey. Alisha publishes her findings and is awarded a generous academic scholarship as a result of her work.

EXAMPLE 3.4
Concurrent Validity: Water Supply

Luis develops an index of overall water supply in desert towns. It is a number based on a mathematical formula that includes average monthly town rainfall, average monthly depth of the town reservoir, and average

Example 3.4 continued

monthly water pressure in the kitchen of the local elementary school. The higher the index, the greater the water supply in the town. Luis collects data for 12 consecutive months and uses his formula to calculate his water supply index. During that year, he also records the number of days each month that the local Department of Water declares as drought days. At the end of the year, Luis plots his index against the number of drought days for each month. He calculates the correlation coefficient between the two data sets to be –0.88. Luis reasons that these two variables should have an inverse relationship, and thus concludes that his index has good criterion validity.

Although it is important to evaluate concurrent validity, you must make sure that you select a gold-standard test that is truly a good criterion against which to judge your new survey instrument. It is not helpful to show good correlations with some obscure index just because it happens to have been published in a journal or book. You should always select gold standards that are relevant, well known, and accepted as being good measures of the variable of interest. When testing concurrent validity, you should select gold standards that have been demonstrated to have psychometric properties of their own. Otherwise, you will be comparing your new scales to a substandard criterion.

Predictive Validity

A survey instrument's **predictive validity** is its usefulness in the forecasting of future events, behaviors, attitudes, or outcomes. Predictive validity may be used during the course of a study to predict response to a stimulus, election winners, success of an intervention, time to a medical end-point, or other objective criteria. Over a brief interval, predictive validity is similar to concurrent validity in that it involves correlating the results of one test with the results of another administered around the same time. If the time frame is longer and the second test occurs much later, then the assessment is of predictive validity. Like concurrent validity, predictive validity is calculated as a correlation coefficient between the initial test and the secondary outcome. Example 3.5 demonstrates that the Pain Tolerance Index that Alisha tested for concurrent validity in Example 3.3 may also be tested for predictive validity.

EXAMPLE 3.5
Predictive Validity: Pain Tolerance

Fourteen years after her initial success, Alisha from Example 3.3 becomes professor of gynecology at a well-respected research university. She decides to use her Pain Tolerance Index to predict narcotic requirements in patients undergoing hysterectomy. Having tested her index for reliability and concurrent validity, she now wants to test it for predictive validity. She administers her index to 100 of her preoperative patients and calculates an index score for each individual. (Recall that a high score reflects a high tolerance for pain.) Once all the surgeries have been completed, Alisha reviews the medical records. She notes the total number of doses of narcotic that were administered for postoperative pain in each patient. She then calculates a correlation coefficient between the two data elements: index score and number of narcotic doses. She finds that the statistic is –0.84. As expected, there is a strong inverse correlation between the Pain Tolerance Index and the amount of narcotic required after surgery. Alisha is pleased to find that her index has high predictive validity in clinical

Example 3.5 continued

practice. She publishes her results in a national medical journal and is later promoted to the position of chief of the department of gynecology at an even more prestigious university.

Continuing with this theme, researchers can use predictive validity in a variety of settings to measure the accuracy of survey instruments. One of the most well-known survey instruments is the Scholastic Assessment Test (formerly the Scholastic Aptitude Test), or the SAT. Example 3.6 illustrates the use of the SAT to predict academic success among a population of college students.

EXAMPLE 3.6
Predictive Validity: SAT Scores

Richard is the dean of students at Shadowmoss College, a small liberal arts school in South Carolina. He decides to look into whether the SAT scores of entering freshmen predict how well the students will perform during their first semester at Shadowmoss. He looks back into the registrar's records for the past 5 years and gathers two data elements for each freshman: SAT score and first-semester grade point average. Richard then directs his assistant, Meryl, to enter the two data sets into a statistical program on her laptop computer and calculate a correlation coefficient between the two. To his surprise, he finds the statistic to be 0.45. The students' SAT scores do not appear to have high predictive validity for early success at Shadowmoss College. He immediately writes a memo to Pamela, the dean of admissions at Shadow-

Example 3.6 continued

moss, to ask that evaluation policies be revised to reflect this important new information.

When Pamela receives Richard's memo, she decides to do a little investigating of her own. She takes Richard's data and splits them out year by year. Using the same formula Meryl used, she calculates correlation coefficients with her own laptop computer and finds that over the past 5 years, the predictive validity of SAT scores has changed; the correlation coefficients for the 5 years, from least to most recent, are 0.21, 0.36, 0.48, 0.57, and 0.72. Pamela writes a memo back to Richard in which she suggests that although SAT scores did not previously have much predictive validity, they have become increasingly more useful for prediction in recent years. Pamela proudly sends a copy of her memo to Chancellor Kara in hopes that the chancellor will take Pamela's work on this subject into consideration when she is making her upcoming decision on who should be promoted to provost.

Predictive validity is one of the most important ways to measure a test's accuracy in practical applications; however, it is seldom used in longitudinal medical experiments that rely on surveys. Because the time frames in such trials are often several years long, secondary interventions may be implemented during a trial to alter the course of a disease or medical condition. If the final outcomes were compared with a test score from the start of the study, their correlation may be diminished. This would falsely decrease the measured predictive validity of the test and perhaps call into question the statistical qualities of an otherwise valid survey instrument.

The situation described in Example 3.6 demonstrates that predictive validity (or any other psychometric statistic) may be used in various ways to support different hypotheses. You must be careful with the conclusions you draw from any of these measured psychometric properties. A good exercise is to ask peers in your area of study who are unfamiliar with your hypothesis to look at a summary of your data and draw conclusions. If enough people draw the same conclusions, you may be somewhat reassured that your inferences are correct. You may also ask peers to take your data and statistics and use them to try to support a point that is opposite to your conclusions. This may open up your mind to different interpretations. It may unhinge your argument, or it may guide your approach to collecting evidence that is less easily refuted.

CONSTRUCT VALIDITY

Construct validity is the most valuable and yet the most difficult way of assessing a survey instrument. It is difficult to understand, to measure, and to report. This form of validity is often determined only after years of experience with a survey instrument. It is a measure of how meaningful the scale or survey instrument is when in practical use. Often, construct validity is not calculated as a quantifiable statistic. Rather, it may be seen as a gestalt of how well a survey instrument performs in a multitude of settings and populations over a number of years. Construct validity is often thought to comprise two other forms of validity: convergent and divergent.

Convergent Validity

Convergent validity implies that several different methods for obtaining the same information about a given trait or concept produce similar results. Evaluating convergent validity is analogous to measuring alternate-form reliability, except that the former is more theoretical and requires a great deal of work, usually by multiple investigators using different approaches.

Divergent Validity

Divergent (or discriminant) **validity** is another theoretically based way of thinking about the ability of a measure to estimate the underlying truth in a given area. For a survey instrument to have divergent validity, it must be shown not to correlate too closely with similar but distinct concepts or traits. This, too, requires much effort over many years of evaluation.

To summarize, testing a survey instrument for construct validity is more like hypothesis testing than like calculating correlation coefficients. Demonstrating construct validity is much more difficult and usually requires a great deal of effort in many different experiments. Construct validity may be said to result from the continued use of a survey instrument to measure some trait, quality, or "construct." Indeed, over a period of years, the survey instrument itself may define the way we think about the variable. It is difficult to present a specific example of construct validity, because its measurement and documentation require such an all-encompassing and multifaceted research strategy.

Type of Validity	Characteristics	Comments
Face	Casual review of how good an item or group of items appears	Assessed by individuals with no formal training in the subject under study
Content	Formal expert review of how good an item or series of items appears	Usually assessed by individuals with expertise in some aspect of the subject under study
Criterion: Concurrent	Measures how well the item or scale correlates with gold-standard measures of the same variable	Requires the identification of an established, generally accepted gold standard
Criterion: Predictive	Measures how well the item or scale predicts expected future observations	Used to predict outcomes or events of significance that the item or scale might subsequently be used to predict
Construct	A theoretical measure of how meaningful a survey instrument is; usually established after years of experience by numerous investigators	Not easily quantifiable

NOTE: Validity is usually expressed as a correlation coefficient, or r value, between two sets of data. Levels of 0.70 or more are generally accepted as representing good validity.

4 Scaling and Scoring

Scales and **indexes** are not merely collections of reliable and valid items about the same topic. In fact, most established scales represent months or years of work spent refining the list of items down to the critical ones that provide a rich view of a single attribute. The most common method used to assess whether different items belong together in a scale is a technique called **factor analysis.** A factor is a hypothetical trait that is thought to be measured by the items in a scale. In factor analysis, a computer-executed algorithm is used to test many different possible combinations of items to determine which of them vary together.

Survey researchers use factor analysis to evaluate and select items from larger pools for inclusion in, or exclusion from, scales or indexes. They then use the resulting scales to produce scores, which in turn are thought to reflect the factors. Factors themselves are theoretical traits or attributes that are only approximated by scales. Researchers sometimes use another advanced, computer-executed technique called **multitrait scaling analysis** to measure how well groups of items hold together as scales.

Example 4.1 provides an illustration of how a researcher might use factor analysis to select items for a scale that purports to measure viewer hostility toward sportscasters during broadcasts of the Olympic Games.

EXAMPLE 4.1
Factor Analysis:
Sportscasters at the Olympics

Kareem works for United Broadcasting Company (UBC) and wishes to measure television viewer hostility toward the sportscasters at Good Broadcasting System (GBS) during that network's coverage of the winter Olympic Games. Kareem knows that viewer hostility will be a difficult concept to define, measure, and package into a scale. He begins by administering a reliable 100-item survey to 350 adult viewers on 10 nights of television coverage during the winter Olympics. The questions include a wide range of viewer responses, including pleasure, boredom, anger, identification with athletes, patriotism, and exasperation.

After the winter Olympics are over, Kareem compiles all his data and works with a statistician to enter them into the mainframe computer at UBC. He performs a factor analysis in which he hypothesizes which items will measure his trait of interest—hostility—as well as various other traits that the survey might measure. The computer puts out a matrix of statistics, called a factor analysis, that examines how well the items hypothesized to measure hostility vary with each other and how well or poorly they vary with the other hypothesized traits. Of the 12 items Kareem has selected, the factor analysis determines that only 7 of them vary together well enough that they can collectively be called a hostility scale. The other 5 turn out to vary more closely with other hypothesized traits. Kareem presents his hostility

Example 4.1 continued

scale to the president of UBC, who must decide how to use it against GBS during negotiations for exclusive rights to the air the upcoming summer Olympic Games.

One popular way of structuring response sets in survey research is the *Likert scale*. This method employs a series of response choices (typically 5) that convey various levels of agreement or disagreement with a statement. For example, the survey instructions might ask a respondent how much he or she agrees with the statement "The hotel guest services were satisfactory." The set of Likert scale responses might be as follows: "strongly agree, somewhat agree, neither agree nor disagree, somewhat disagree, strongly disagree." Or an item reading, "How often do you feel your self-esteem is low?" might have a Likert scale response set that reads, "all of the time, much of the time, about half the time, a little of the time, none of the time." (There are numerous other ways to structure response sets; these are discussed more fully in **How to Ask Survey Questions**, Volume 2 in this series.)

Scoring a survey instrument is usually fairly straightforward and amenable to the creation of computer-driven algorithms. Most established survey instruments have published scoring manuals that instruct the user on how many points to count for each response to each item. When you are using an established instrument, it is important that you read the scoring rules carefully, because there are many different ways to convert raw scores to standardized scale scores. This allows researchers to compare different populations from different studies. In some survey instruments, a high score is better, whereas in others, a high score is worse. Some are converted to a standard 0-100 range; others may use a range that goes from 0 to 1, 4, 25, and so on.

When you are creating a set of scoring rules for a new survey instrument, you must determine whether to use a sum, an average, or another formula to derive the scale score. Because different items may have 2, 3, 4, 5, or more responses, you must decide whether to value each response or each item the same.

EXAMPLE 4.2
Scoring: Beach Quality

To gather information that will help them select a site for next year's beachfront intramural volleyball tournament, Fred and Barney design a new 2-item index that measures the quality of different beaches. The items and the numbers of points for the responses are as follows:

Circle one number for each item.

1. The average summer temperature at this beach is

   < 70° 0
   70°-80° 1
   > 80° 2

2. The average number of clear days per summer month at this beach is

   < 7 0
   7 to 13 1
   14 to 20 2
   21 to 25 3
   > 25 4

After testing the reliability and validity of the survey instrument extensively at various sample beaches, Fred and Barney are satisfied that it is both reliable and valid. However, they disagree on how to carry out the scoring. Fred wants to score the index by summing the total

Example 4.2 continued

number of points in both of the items and then dividing by 6 (the perfect total score). Barney wants to score the index by calculating the percentage scores for both of the items and then averaging them together. Barney would divide the number of points in Item 1 by 2 (a perfect score for that item), divide the number of points in Item 2 by 4 (a perfect score for that item), and then calculate a mean score for the two items. Both Fred's and Barney's scores would be reported on 100-point scales, but they would be calculated differently. To see whether the results from the two methods would be different, Fred and Barney convince the tournament administrator to fly them to Cape Cod, Massachusetts, for a trial.

While on Cape Cod, Fred and Barney travel to Provincetown and rate the beach at Herring Cove with scores of 2 and 3, respectively, for the two items. By Fred's scoring method, Herring Cove would score $(2 + 3) / 6 = 83$ (on a 100-point scale). By Barney's method, Herring Cove would score $[(2 / 2) + (3 / 4)] / 2 = 88$.

The reason Barney's method yields a higher score is that he values both items equally by scoring them individually and averaging the item results. Herring Cove has a perfect score on Item 1, and Barney's method values Item 1 more highly. Fred's method values each item response, not each item, equally. Therefore, the responses in Item 1 are relatively discounted in the total score.

Example 4.2 shows how using different scoring techniques can produce very different survey results from the same data. This example shows that seemingly subtle alterations in scoring methods can lead to significant differences in scale scores. Both Fred's and Barney's methods are correct, but they place different values on the items. When designing a scoring system for a new survey instrument, you must recognize these differences and plan accordingly. Remember, if you score a scale by simply adding up the total number of points from each item, those items with larger response sets will be valued relatively higher than those with smaller response sets. One way of avoiding this problem and valuing all responses equally is to assign increased points to each response in items with smaller response sets. This common technique is demonstrated in Example 4.3.

EXAMPLE 4.3
Beach Quality Revisited

After much discussion, Barney wins the scoring debate with Fred, and they decide to score their 2-item beach quality index in a manner that confers equal weight to each item. The scoring system they produce is as follows:

	Response	Points Counted
Item 1	0	0
	1	25
	2	50
Item 2	0	0
	1	12.5
	2	25
	3	37.5
	4	50

With this method, scoring is accomplished simply through the summing of the total number of assigned points for each response. The Herring Cove beach from Example 4.2 would be scored by adding 50 (Item 1 = 2) and 37.5 (Item 2 = 3) to yield a total score of 87.5, which we round to 88, the exact same answer as Barney got in Example 4.2.

5
Creating and Using a Codebook

In survey research, coding includes the process of going through each respondent's questionnaire and looking for conflicting answers, missing data, handwritten notes, and other variations from desired "circle one answer" responses. Before you can enter the survey responses onto a data tape or into a computer file for analysis, you must decide how you are going to categorize any ambiguous answers. No matter how clearly you spell out the instructions to respondents to "circle only one answer for each item," you will have unclear responses to some items. Some respondents may not follow instructions for skip patterns correctly, and some may circle more than one answer in response sets that are supposed to be mutually exclusive and collectively exhaustive. No matter how thoroughly you think through your items and response sets before you test your survey, issues will always arise during data collection that will require you to make subjective decisions or corrections. Of course, maintaining a **codebook** is greatly facilitated by the use of a computer- or Internet-based tracking system. Example 5.1 shows one coding issue that came up during a recent survey on family support systems.

EXAMPLE 5.1
How Many Kids?

In a recent self-administered survey concerning family support systems for men with emphysema, one seemingly straightforward question caused a moderate amount of confusion in several respondents. The item read:

How many of your children under age 18 live in your home?

None 0
1 1
2 to 4 2
More than 4 3

Three respondents answered *none,* but then wrote in the margin that two to four of their wives' school-age children from previous marriages lived in the home. During the coding of this survey, the researchers decided to count the wives' young children, because stepchildren in the home fulfill a role similar enough to that of biological children that there should be no distinction in this study. The research context determined how these children were classified. If the same item had appeared on a survey assessing male fertility, it would not have been appropriate to include the stepchildren. The researchers recorded their decision in the study's codebook for future reference.

The most common data problem arises from the fact that respondents often skip items, either intentionally or by mistake. Usually, you will have to code those items as missing data and decide later how to treat them in the analysis. Occasionally, you can infer the answer to an item from other responses or from other sources, particularly if it is a sociodemographic item, such as age. The best way to handle missing data is to contact the respondent and ask for the answer to the skipped item. However, this is not always possible. Example 5.2 demonstrates one way to attempt to solve the problem of missing data.

EXAMPLE 5.2
Missing Data

In the survey described in Example 5.1, concerning family support systems for men with emphysema, the researchers included the following item on family outings:

During the past 4 weeks, how often did you and *all* the other family members who live in your home go out to dinner together?

Not at all 0
Once or twice 1
Three to five times 2
Six or more times. 3

After all the surveys had been returned, they were coded by an undergraduate student research assistant, who found that 15 respondents had failed to answer this item at all. When he reported this to the study's principal investigator, she asked him to telephone these 15 respondents to try to fill in the missing data. Only 9 of the respondents were available and provided answers to this item; 6 were not reachable, despite numerous attempts. The researchers recorded information about the telephone follow-up in the study codebook for future reference.

Missing data constitute one of the most problematic areas in survey research. It is critically important that you make extensive efforts to minimize the amount of data missing from your survey, because missing data detract from the overall quality of the survey results. The fact that data are missing should also serve to alert you to the possibility that your research methods need a quality check: The more data are missing, the poorer the quality of the methodology.

Data may be missing for a variety of reasons. For example, respondents may omit data intentionally or because they have misunderstood skip patterns, failed to grasp the language used, been unable to read the type, or grown tired of a lengthy survey. Whatever the explanation, missing data can be devastating to an otherwise well-planned survey project.

Example 5.3 demonstrates the value of the codebook when a surveyor makes a decision regarding data after the data have been collected but before they are coded on the survey.

EXAMPLE 5.3
Counting Homicides

Sheila performed a review of police records in the 50 largest cities in North America during the past 3 years to identify crime rates. One of the variables she collected was the total number of homicides in each city during each year. She found the homicide counts to range from zero to 1,045. During the data collection stage of her project, Sheila decided to enter the exact number on a blank line next to the question. Later, when she coded the surveys, she decided to collapse the homicide counts into six groups that she felt were meaningful:

Number of Homicides	Response Code
0	1
1-10	2
11-50	3
51-100	4
101-250	5
> 250	6

Example 5.3 continued

Sheila made a research decision that she did not need to analyze her data based on the exact number of homicides. She recorded the above table in her study codebook for future reference. She knew that if she decided to add more cities to her series several years later, she would not be able to remember where she had drawn the lines between groups. She also knew that she would be able to refer to her thorough codebook to get that information.

In some senses, the codebook is a log or documentation of the research decisions that are made during the coding or review of surveys. Despite your best efforts, you will be unable to remember all the small decisions that you make along the way in carrying out the collection, processing, and analysis of survey data. The codebook is a summary of all those decisions. It functions not only as a record but also as a rule book for future analyses using the same or similar data.

The importance of keeping meticulous records cannot be overemphasized. Inevitably, in survey research, questions arise about how you collected a data element, where you went for resources, how you documented certain variables, whether you completed follow-up in a certain way, and so on. The only way to guarantee that you can reproduce your methods accurately is to maintain excellent records. This includes your codebook as well as records of the way you structured each aspect of your methodology and data analysis.

6 Pilot Testing

Before a new feature film appears in movie theaters, the movie's producers often show it to sample audiences in various cities to observe their reactions to the characters, plot, ending, and other aspects of the entertainment experience. If these sample audiences consistently dislike some aspect of the film, it is usually changed before the movie is released. Similarly, before a new product is introduced into retail stores, the manufacturer always test-markets it to gauge consumer satisfaction. And before you buy a new car, you almost always take it for a test drive, even if you feel certain about your choice of models.

In survey research, **pilot testing**, or pretesting the survey instrument with a small sample population, serves a function similar to these other kinds of tests. Pilot testing is one of the most important stages in the development of a new survey instrument, and time and again you will find that it proves to be worth the energy you spend on it. Pilot testing has three main benefits:

- It helps you to identify errors in the survey.

- It allows you to learn where your survey instrument may need redesign.

- It predicts possible problems you may encounter in using the instrument.

Pilot testing almost always identifies errors in a survey's form and presentation. Inevitably, despite extensive thought and planning, errors occur in the final versions of questionnaires. They range from confusing typographical mistakes to overlapping response sets to ambiguous instructions. When you are creating a survey instrument, you are usually so close to the project that you may overlook even the most obvious errors. Pilot testing allows you a chance to correct these errors before the survey is mass-produced or used on a wider scope to gather real data. It allows you the time and opportunity to redesign any problematic parts of the survey before it is actually used. Pilot testing also predicts difficulties that may arise during subsequent data collection that might otherwise have gone unnoticed. At this early stage, most problems are still correctable.

Sometimes the issues identified during pilot testing are problems of form. For older respondents, many of whom may have impaired vision, the type size and font are especially important. Pilot testing may also expose respondents' difficulties with the reading comprehension level of the survey. Many survey respondents are less technically educated than survey researchers. If a survey is written at a level above the understanding of the intended respondents, the resulting data will be spurious or incomplete. Respondents must be able to understand the semantics of the survey items in order to provide honest and thoughtful answers. The general rule is that surveys should be written at no higher than a sixth-grade reading level. Software applications are available that can help you to estimate the reading level of your survey. Likewise, many populations today are not homogeneous in their primary language. Even if a survey is written at a comprehensible level for native English speakers, individuals who are not completely fluent in or comfortable with English may answer with data that are not usable.

Language may present significant challenges, but just because your intended respondents do not speak English fluently, that does not mean you cannot gather data from them. If there is information that you want to gather that is available reliably and validly only in the respondents' native tongue, and if you are very industrious, you may undertake the creation of a foreign-language version of your survey.

In addition, pilot testing can help you to make sure that the items in your survey are culturally sensitive. Certain areas that are covered in a questionnaire may represent concepts that are unfamiliar to some respondents. Pilot testing allows you to identify many such potential impediments in advance, so you can correct them before you have expended too many resources. (For discussion of how you can avoid the pitfalls associated with crossing cultural and language barriers in survey research, see Chapters 7 and 8).

Pilot testing will not eliminate any of the problems mentioned above, but it will allow you to identify them so that you can consider the implications and decide prospectively how to handle them.

Example 6.1 illustrates one of the simple but common problems often identified during pilot testing of a survey. When designing questionnaire layout, many researchers are tempted to squeeze as many items as possible onto one or two pages. They think that if a survey looks short, their respondents will believe it to be easy and quick to complete. But shortening the length of a questionnaire by making the type size smaller only makes it more difficult to read. If respondents have trouble just reading the words on the page, they will not have much energy left to think about the meaning of the questions. Ramon in Example 6.1 learned that sometimes a survey that is a little longer but much easier to read can yield more valuable results than one that fits nicely into a short format and is difficult to read. Two pages are effectively shorter than one if the type is easier to read.

One trick that some researchers use is the creative numbering of items. Instead of simply numbering every question

EXAMPLE 6.1
Type Size

Ramon was very pleased that his new 10-item question-naire on attitudes toward aging fit onto one side of a single page. He estimated that it should require about 5 minutes to complete. Before Ramon set out to assess his survey's reliability and validity in a sample of 250 older New Yorkers, his professor urged him to conduct a small pilot test with six senior citizens. Ramon set up the pilot test by calling the activities office of a local community senior center and recruiting volunteers.

On the appointed date, the four women and two men met Ramon at the community center for the short pilot test. To his surprise, Ramon found that the average time they took to fill out his survey was 20 minutes. When he queried them as to why, five of the six stated that they had a great deal of trouble reading the questions, even with their glasses. They had no problems with reading comprehension or with English; they simply could not see the type on the page clearly.

Ramon revised the type size on his survey from 8-point to 12-point. Instead of fitting onto a single page, the survey now took up two pages. Ramon mailed the new version to his six pilot-test respondents and asked for their comments. All of them replied that it was now much easier to read and fill out.

from 1 to whatever, they break items up into groups or sections to create the illusion that the survey is shorter than it really is. If several items in a survey rely on the same response set, you can make them appear as a single item with several subitems. Rather than numbering each item separately, you number the instruction and define the items with letters. This technique is demonstrated in Example 6.2.

EXAMPLE 6.2
Arizona Geological Survey

Marissa and Jacob are geology students who wish to collect data on the types of rocks found in the various counties of Arizona. They design a 40-item questionnaire to be completed by the interior commissioners of all the counties, but they know that these individuals are quite busy and may not want to take the time to fill out a lengthy survey. Marissa and Jacob do some basic research and discover that by far the three most common rock forms in the state are quartz, limestone, and shale. Before sending out their survey, they perform a pilot test with two of the commissioners they know personally. They learn that the commissioners' main complaint about the survey is that 40 items seem like quite a lot.

Because they do not want to delete any of the items, Marissa and Jacob carefully craft a survey format that relies heavily on groupings of similar items. In the cover letter they send out with the questionnaires, they introduce their research project and ask for the commissioners' help in complying with a "short 10-item survey." The survey's first item is as follows:

Example 6.2 continued

1. Please circle the number corresponding to the most common type of rock at each of these sites in your county.	Quartz	Limestone	Shale
a. Lakes	1	2	3
b. Hills	1	2	3
c. Mountains	1	2	3
d. Suburbs	1	2	3
e. Forests	1	2	3
f. Riverbeds	1	2	3

By combining their items together into groups as shown above, Marissa and Jacob were able to reduce 40 items to 10 items without shortening their survey at all. It simply appears shorter. Marissa and Jacob hope that the county interior commissioners will be cooperative in filling out this "short" questionnaire despite their busy schedules.

Surveys do not have to be filled with page after page of boring and monotonous questions. You can spice up the demeanor of your survey instrument by using some very simple techniques. Varying the response sets into columns for like groups, as in Example 6.2, is one commonly used method. Another is the incorporation of graphics into the response sets. To provide mental breaks for your respondents, you can place a few short, easy questions after series of more difficult questions.

Skip patterns are another area of questionnaire design that presents challenges for survey researchers. Using instructions such as "If you answered yes to the previous question, then skip to page 4" may be a wonderful way to use the same questionnaire for different groups, but it may cause you and your respondents untold frustration and can lead to devastating amounts of missing data. Often, pilot testing will help you to identify problems with skip patterns and other simple visual problems with your survey's layout and format. At this stage, you can easily correct what is wrong and then retest the instrument before you proceed to your primary effort at data collection. Example 6.3 illustrates the problem of confusing skip patterns. As the example shows, online and computer-aided survey instruments allow you to tailor the presentation of items and to incorporate skip patterns much more unobtrusively than you can in pen-and-paper surveys.

EXAMPLE 6.3
Algebra Attitudes

Estelle wishes to survey the attitudes of ninth-grade students in Chicago toward different approaches to learning math. She designs a comprehensive questionnaire with several branch points that direct students to different sets of questions. The first item in the questionnaire is as follows:

Example 6.3 continued

1. Would you prefer to learn algebra by

Listening to a teacher
present new material
and work problems . . . . A

Listening to a teacher,
but working problems on your own . . . . . . B

Reading new material
and working problems all on your own C

If you answered A, continue with item 2, but skip items 12-36, and then complete items 37-50. If you answered B, skip items 2-11, continue with items 12-23, skip items 24-36, but complete items 37-50. If you answered C, skip items 2-23, but complete items 24-50.

Before taking her survey into the entire school district, Estelle pilot-tested it in her daughter's ninth-grade class of 30 girls and boys. She found that the students had numerous questions about the skip patterns. Despite their best efforts, they simply found the instructions too confusing. Estelle was forced to take her survey back to the drawing board to make it more user-friendly for these respondents. She was able to design an online version that presented the appropriate next item each time an item was answered, so the respondents did not have to deal directly with the skip patterns. When she returned to the same class to repeat her pilot test, she found that the students logged on and sailed through the survey without any apparent difficulty.

Pilot testing is not limited to new survey instruments. It is beneficial to perform pilot tests even when you are using often-published and well-established survey instruments. Unless you are working with a population that is exactly the same as the other populations in which a survey instrument has been validated, you will probably be introducing some new twist in your particular sample. Pilot-testing established survey instruments is extraordinarily helpful in all survey research. You may find that, for whatever reason, even an established survey instrument does not perform well in your pilot-test sample. This will afford you the opportunity to select a different survey instrument or even develop your own if you have the time and resources to do so. Example 6.4 provides an illustration of a case in which pilot testing revealed that an established survey instrument was not relevant for the population of interest.

EXAMPLE 6.4
Type A Personalities

The Jenkins Activity Scale is a published and well-established survey instrument that distinguishes individuals with relatively high levels of daily anxiety and compulsiveness, so-called Type A personalities, from those with lower levels of stress, so-called Type B personalities. It is intended to identify people at risk for heart attacks, strokes, and high blood pressure.

In an effort to find potential clients with certain investment habits, the marketing director at a money management firm of dubious reputation decided to mail the Jenkins Activity Scale, which is a self-administered instrument, to a national sample of 5,000 members of the American Association of Retired Persons (AARP). The marketing director had an idea that Type B personalities would be more likely than Type A personalities to hand over their savings for investment without asking too

Example 6.4 continued

many questions. After a thorough literature review, the marketing director selected the Jenkins Activity Survey because it is short and easily scored, and its reliability and validity are well documented. The marketing director submitted a proposal concerning the use of the survey to the firm's vice president for marketing.

Before committing the firm's resources to conducting a survey using this particular survey instrument, the vice president asked her assistant to conduct a small pilot test by sending the Jenkins Activity Survey to 12 members of the local AARP chapter. Of the 8 surveys that were returned, 7 of the respondents had completed only a small fraction of the items. It turned out that most of the items on the survey referred to the respondent's conduct at work, interactions with professional colleagues, and number of vacation days taken from the job. Of the 8 people who participated in the pilot test, only 1 was currently employed. The remainder were retired and could not answer many of the questions—not surprising, given the target audience of retired persons.

The vice president fired the marketing director and hired an expensive outside consulting firm to develop and evaluate psychometrically a new survey instrument that assesses daily anxiety levels in retired persons as a predictor of investment strategies.

Pilot testing is a necessary and important part of survey development. It provides you with useful information about how your survey instrument actually plays in the field. Although performing a pilot test requires extra time and energy, it is a critical step in assessing the practical application of your survey instrument.

Checklist for Pilot Testing

✓ Are there any typographical errors or misspelled words in the instrument?

✓ Do the item numbers make sense?

✓ Is the type size big enough to be read easily?

✓ Is the vocabulary appropriate for the respondents?

✓ Is the survey too long?

✓ Are the styles of the items too monotonous?

✓ Are there easy questions mixed in with the difficult questions?

✓ Are the skip patterns too difficult to follow?

✓ Does the survey format flow well?

✓ Are the items appropriate for the respondents?

✓ Are the items sensitive to possible cultural barriers?

✓ Is the survey in the best language for the respondents?

 **Multicultural Issues**

$\mathbf{W}$hen you are designing new survey instruments or applying established ones in populations of different ethnicities, creeds, or nationalities, you must make sure that your items translate well into both the language and the culture of your target audience. Although you may be able to translate a survey instrument's items into a new language, you may find that they do not measure the same dimension in different cultures. This is particularly relevant when you are studying social attitudes and health behaviors. Different cultures have very different concepts of health, well-being, illness, and disease, for example. A concept that is well developed in one culture may not even exist in another. Even if you start with a well-validated survey instrument in English, you need to be aware that various populations within the United States and elsewhere in the world may not approach the concepts it measures with the same ideas.

Failure to be attentive to multicultural issues may result in significant bias in the collection of data. For example, when classifying ethnicities, many survey researchers categorize all Asians together. For some projects, this may be acceptable, but many attitudes and behaviors vary a great deal among Chinese, Japanese, Filipino, Korean, and other cultures within Asia. If you lump all such ethnicities into one class, you may overlook differences that are important to your conclusions.

Example 7.1 illustrates how problems can arise not only from language barriers but also from conceptual differences due to culture.

EXAMPLE 7.1
Elderly Women

Olivia decided to use an established, well-validated 24-item survey instrument to measure family attitudes in elderly American women of Anglo and Latino descent. In order to facilitate her survey's crossing the potential language barrier, Olivia asked her friend Juanita, a native Mexican, to translate the survey into Spanish. After the translation was complete, Olivia administered the instrument to a sample of 300 elderly women, of whom 150 classified themselves as Latina and 150 classified themselves as Anglo.

After she tabulated her data, Olivia was disappointed to discover that, despite the perfect translation into Spanish, the Latina respondents' surveys were missing a tremendous amount of data. When she researched the matter more closely, Olivia realized that she had failed to take into account the multicultural issues raised by her project. She found out that the Latinas had a concept of family that was completely different from that of the Anglo-American women. For example, the Anglos tended to include only parents and children in their concept of family, whereas the Latinas tended to consider grandparents, aunts and uncles, and cousins as well. The survey instrument had been validated only in Anglo-American populations. Although the words in the survey had been translated quite well into Spanish, the philosophies of family in the two groups were so different that most of the Anglo concepts had no real meaning to the Latinas. Therefore, they left many items blank, and Olivia was unable to analyze her data in a useful way.

8 Translations

Translating a survey into a foreign language is not as simple as Olivia in Example 7.1 thought. You must consider not only issues of culture, but also issues of linguistics. The correct way to translate your survey is to start by identifying two or three bilingual individuals and having them perform independent "forward translations" into the new language. Next, you have these translators reconcile any differences in word choices in the new language. You then find two or three more bilingual individuals and have them perform independent "back-translations" in which they convert the original reconciled translation back into English. Next, you have one or two bilingual individuals perform independent reviews of the forward, reconciled, and back-translated versions in order to iron out any language differences and agree on the final wording of each item in the new language. Finally, after you pilot-test the instrument with a few bilingual subjects, you conduct a larger-scale test to measure the instrument's reliability and validity in the new language (see Examples 8.1 and 8.2).

EXAMPLE 8.1
How Often in Spanish

Recently, while testing a linguistic translation of a survey instrument designed to measure symptoms in men with chronic prostatitis, researchers collected data from many Spanish-speaking patients, including 15 in Argentina, 15 in Mexico, 4 in the United States, and 3 in Spain. The translation had high overall reliability, but the respondents noted that they had difficulty distinguishing between the response categories *a menudo* (*often*) and *normalmente* (*usually*) in one of the items. The researchers decided to revise *a menudo* to *muchas veces* (*much of the time*) and *normalmente* to *casi siempre* (*almost always*) to improve the distinctiveness of the response categories.

EXAMPLE 8.2
Pain in Spanish

The original English version of the survey described in Example 8.1 contained the phrase *pain or discomfort* six times. The recommended translation was *dolor o incomodidad,* which was back-translated as *pain or discomfort.* However, one reviewer noted that *incomodidad* is not generally used in the medical sense, and that *molestia,* which was also back-translated as *pain or discomfort,* conveyed the proper meaning in the medical sense. The other reviewers agreed. The final Spanish-language version of the survey used the phrase *dolor o molestia,* which seemed to be the simplest and most appropriate translation for the medical context.

Exercises

1. Northwest Cable administers a television preference survey to 100 viewers in the company's
   southeast region and includes the following two
   items at different points in the same questionnaire:

   - How many hours of TV did you watch in the past 7
     days?

   - How many programs of what length did you watch
     during the past 7 days?

   Which of the following is the company trying to
   document?

   a. Alternate-form reliability
   b. Test-retest reliability
   c. Internal consistency reliability
   d. All of the above

2. Southwest Cable administers a new television
   preference questionnaire to 50 viewers in the
   company's northeast region on January 15, then
   repeats the identical survey with the same 50
   viewers on February 15 and finds close correla-

tions between the two data sets. Southwest Cable's survey instrument can be said to have good

    a. Alternate-form reliability
    b. Test-retest reliability
    c. Internal consistency reliability
    d. All of the above

3. When you read that a scale has a coefficient alpha of 0.90, you can be assured that the scale is a high degree of

    a. Alternate-form reliability
    b. Test-retest reliability
    c. Internal consistency reliability
    d. Concurrent validity

4. Suppose you are developing a measure of student satisfaction with school lunches in a 750-student elementary school. How might you design an experiment to assess test-retest reliability?

5. Design two different response sets to test alternate-form reliability for the following item from a meteorological survey instrument about regional precipitation:

> *How much rain did your region have during the past 4 weeks?*

6. A new survey instrument is published for assessing safety in automobiles. It includes 12 items about a wide range of qualities, such as strength of the seat belt straps, the temperature at which the engine overheats, how the windshield shatters during impact, thickness of the steel in the doors, and adequacy of the ventilation system. The survey instrument is tested with several

models of cars, and it is determined that it has good test-retest and alternate-form reliability, but its coefficient alpha is only 0.23. What does this mean?

7. The housing office of a large university wants to measure student satisfaction with various aspects of the campus dormitories. After researching the relevant published literature, the housing director cannot find a survey instrument that she thinks is appropriate, so she decides to develop her own. She remembers from her survey research course in college that her index must be reliable and valid. She also remembers that her index must have good content validity. How would you advise her to begin her project?

8. Brian has designed and pilot-tested a new 20-item self-administered survey instrument that measures religious observance in a group of mid-westerners. How might he go about assessing it for concurrent validity?

9. Obsessions Unlimited is a company that provides personal organization services; customers pay a fee in return for receiving individualized help in organizing their personal lives. The company is looking for a better way to assess the quality of applicants for employment as personal organization assistants. The director of personnel wants to devise a screening questionnaire that has excellent predictive validity in selecting persons for employment as personal organizational assistants who will produce customer satisfaction. He puts together a reliable self-administered index of 20 items that job applicants can complete easily. How should he test his index's predictive validity?

ANSWERS

1. Alternate-form reliability

2. Test-retest reliability

3. All of the above

4. Because the students' satisfaction with particular lunches may be different on different days, you must administer your survey at separate times on the same afternoon after lunchtime. For example, you might have students complete questionnaires right after they have had lunch and then again right before school lets out.

5. *Response Set 1:* In this region, the average total rainfall (to the nearest 10th of an inch) during the past 4 weeks was

> None
> 0.1 to 4 inches
> 4.1 to 8 inches
> 8.1 to 12 inches
> More than 12 inches

Response Set 2: In this region, the number of days it rained during the past 4 weeks was

> No days
> 1-7 days
> 8-14 ays
> 15-21 days
> 22-28 days

Response Set 3: In this region, rainfall during the past 4 weeks has been

Below average for this time of year
About average for this time of year
Above average for this time of year

6. The survey instrument has low internal consistency reliability. This means that although the items seem to focus on various aspects of the same concept, they may actually be quite different. The author should consider the possibility that the items may not be measuring the same concept.

7. If she wants to ensure content validity, she must tailor her survey instrument to the needs of the students themselves. The best way to start would be to put together a focus group of students currently living in the campus dorms. During this exploratory session, she could get an idea of what issues are important to the students. She might then put together a first draft of her questionnaire and show it to these students for their comments. This would provide initial testing of content validity.

8. In order to assess concurrent validity, Brian must identify some gold-standard method of assessing religious observance. He should start by looking in the sociology research literature. There may not be any such established measure, however, so he may have to select a measure that appears to be a gold standard. For example, he might use actual attendance at religious services or religious functions during a 4-week period for a randomly selected group of midwesterners.

9. In order to test the predictive validity of his screening questionnaire, the personnel director must also select an established outcome measure

of customer satisfaction. He should administer his questionnaire to all employment applicants over a defined period of time. He should then use the selected outcome measure to document the satisfaction of those customers served by the different employees. By using the results from the screening index to try to predict which employees will have good results on the satisfaction outcomes measure, he can assess the predictive validity of his questionnaire. If those who score well on the screening index also score well on the satisfaction index, then his screening index can be said to have good predictive validity.

Suggested Readings

Coons, S. J., Rao, S., Keininger, D. L., & Hays, R. D. (2000). A comparative review of generic quality-of-life instruments. *PharmacoEconomics, 17,* 13-35.

Guyatt, G. H., Kirshner, B., & Jaeschke, R. (1992). Measuring health status: What are the necessary measurement properties? *Journal of Clinical Epidemiology, 45,* 1341-1345.

Hays, R. D., Sherbourne, C. D., & Mazel, R. M. (1993). The RAND 36-Item Health Survey 1.0. *Health Economics, 2,* 217-227.

Hays, R. D., & Woolley, J. M. (2000). The concept of clinically meaningful difference in health-related quality-of-life research: How meaningful is it? *PharmacoEconomics, 18,* 419-423.

Kagawa-Singer, M., & Blackhall, L. J. (2001). Negotiating cross-cultural issues at the end of life: "You got to go where he lives." *Journal of the American Medical Association, 286,* 2993-3001.

Kaplan, R. (1990). Utility assessment for estimating quality-adjusted life years. In F. Sloan (Ed.), *Valuing health care: Costs, benefits, and effectiveness of pharmaceuticals and other medical technologies* (pp. 31-60). Boston: Cambridge University Press.

Litwin, M. S., Hays, R. D., Fink, A., Ganz, P. A., Leake, B., Leach, G. E., & Brook, R. H. (1995). Quality-of-life outcomes in men treated for localized prostate cancer. *Journal of the American Medical Association, 273,* 129-135.

Reiser, S. J. (1993). The era of the patient: Using the experience of illness in shaping the missions of health care. *Journal of the American Medical Association, 269,* 1012-1017.

Rossi, P. H., Wright, J. D., & Anderson, A. B. (Eds.). (1983). *Handbook of survey research.* San Diego, CA: Academic Press.

Slevin, M. L., Plant, H., Lynch, D., Drinkwater, J., & Gregory, W. M. (1988). Who should measure quality of life, the doctor or the patient? *British Journal of Cancer, 57,* 109-112.

Ware, J. E., Jr., Kosinski, M., Gandek, B., Aaronson, N. K., Apolone, G., Bech, P., et al. (1998). The factor structure of the SF-36 Health Survey in 10 countries: Results from the IQOLA Project. *Journal of Clinical Epidemiology, 51,* 1159-1165.

Ware, J. E., Jr., Kosinski, M., & Keller, S. D. (1994). *SF-36 physical and mental health summary scales: A user's manual.* Boston: New England Medical Center, Health Institute.

Ware, J. E., Jr., Kosinski, M., & Keller, S. D. (1996). A 12-item short-form health survey: Construction of scales and preliminary tests of reliability and validity. *Medical Care, 34,* 220-233.

Ware, J. E., Jr., & Sherbourne, C. D. (1992). The MOS 36-Item Short-Form Health Survey (SF-36): I. Conceptual framework and item selection. *Medical Care, 30,* 473-483.

Glossary

Alternate-form reliability—A measure of survey reproducibility in which an item and/or response set is worded in two or more different ways and the different versions are compared for consistency in responses.

Codebook—A collection of rules developed during the translation of survey responses into numerical codes for analysis. For example, a codebook might contain a rule on ethnicity that assigns the number 1 to African Americans, 2 to Anglos, 3 to Asians, 4 to Latinos, and so on. Another rule might assign the number 9 to all items for which data are missing. The codebook is a summary of all such rules to be used as a reference during data analysis.

Concurrent validity—A measure of survey accuracy in which the results of a new survey or scale are compared with the results from a generally accepted gold-standard test after both tests are administered to the same group of respondents.

Construct validity—A theoretical gestalt-type measure of how meaningful a survey instrument is, usually after many years of experience by numerous investigators in many varied settings.

Content validity—A measure of survey accuracy that involves formal review by individuals who are experts in the subject matter of the survey.

Convergent validity—A measure of survey accuracy that involves using different tools to obtain information about a particular variable and seeing how well the results correlate. Evaluating convergent validity is analogous to measuring alternate-form reliability, but with different established instruments rather than different wordings of single items.

Correlation coefficient—A statistical measure of how closely two variables or measures are related to each other. Correlation coefficients are usually calculated and reported as r values.

Criterion validity—A measure of survey accuracy that involves comparing the survey to other tests. Criterion validity may be categorized as convergent or divergent.

Divergent validity—A measure of survey accuracy that involves using different tools for obtaining information about similar but discrete variables and seeing if they differ.

Face validity—The most casual measure of a survey's accuracy, usually assessed informally by nonexperts.

Factor analysis—A computer-assisted method of analysis used to assess whether different items on a survey belong together in one scale.

Index—See **Scale.**

Internal consistency reliability—A measure of survey accuracy that reflects how well different items in a scale vary together when applied to a group of respondents.

Interobserver reliability—The reproducibility of a set of observations on one variable made by different observers.

Intraobserver reliability—The reproducibility of a set of observations on one variable made by the same observer at different times.

Item—A question that appears on a survey or in an index.

Measurement error—The degree to which instruments yield data that are incorrect due to the measurement process.

Multitrait scaling analysis—An advanced computer-assisted method of measuring how well various items go together in a particular scale (similar to factor analysis).

Pilot testing—The practice of trying out a survey or index during the development phase with a small sample one or more times to see how well the survey works, to expose errors, and to identify areas of difficulty for respondents.

Practice effect—A phenomenon in which a respondent becomes familiar with items on a survey or index taken at several time points. Over time, the individual's responses correlate highly with each other simply because he or she is remembering previous answers, and not because the variable being measured is unchanged.

Predictive validity—A measure of survey accuracy in which an item or scale is correlated with future observations of behavior, survey responses, or other events.

Psychometrics—The science of measuring psychological or qualitative phenomena.

r **value**—The statistic that is used to report correlations. See **Correlation coefficient.**

Random error—The degree to which instruments yield data that are incorrect *not* due to the measurement process, but due to uncontrollable fluctuations in responses.

Reliability—The reproducibility or stability of data or observations. When using a survey or index, one wants to achieve high reliability, which implies that the data are highly reproducible.

GLOSSARY

Scale—A series of items measuring a single variable, trait, or domain.

Scaling—A process in which different items are placed together in a single index that pertains to one variable of interest. This process often involves factor analysis and multitrait scaling analysis.

Scoring—The conversion of an individual's survey answers into a numerical value for comparison with the answers of other individuals or of the same individual at different times.

Split-halves method—A technique used to assess alternate-form reliability in which a large sample is divided equally into two smaller samples, each of the two halves of the sample are administered different forms of the same question, and the responses of the two halves of the sample are compared. See **Alternate-form reliability.**

Survey instrument (or Survey)—A series of items that typically contains several scales. A survey may be self-administered or may require a trained interviewer. It may be very long or contain a single item. It may be about issues as personal as sexual function or as impersonal as rainfall.

Test-retest reliability—A measure of the stability of responses over time in the same group of respondents. Many investigators report test-retest reliability by administering the same survey at two different time points (often 4 weeks apart) to the same group of individuals.

Validity—An assessment of how well a survey or index measures what it is intended to measure.

About the Author

Mark S. Litwin, M.D., M.P.H., is Professor of Health Services and Urology at the UCLA School of Public Health and the David Geffen School of Medicine at UCLA, where he teaches and conducts outcomes research and practices urologic oncology. He received his M.D. from Emory University and trained in urology at Harvard Medical School's Brigham and Women's Hospital. He obtained his M.P.H. from UCLA, where he was a Robert Wood Johnson Clinical Scholar. In 2001, he received the Gold Cystoscope Award, the American Urological Association's highest honor for the academic contributions of a young investigator. He has extensive experience in health services research, including studies concerning health-related quality of life, patient utilities, quality of care, and medical resource use. His research is funded by the NIH, the American Cancer Society, and the California Department of Health Services.